Contents

Greece

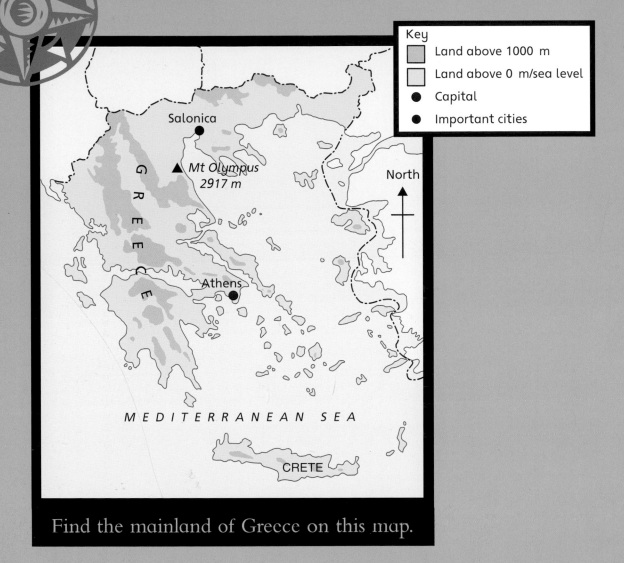

Key
- ◻ Land above 1000 m
- ◻ Land above 0 m/sea level
- ● Capital
- ● Important cities

Salonica

▲ Mt Olympus 2917 m

North

Athens

GREECE

MEDITERRANEAN SEA

CRETE

Find the mainland of Greece on this map.

Greece is the furthest south of all countries in **Europe**. Most of the **mainland** is surrounded by the Mediterranean Sea. It also has about 2000 islands of all sizes.

A beach in Greece.

People live on only 160 of the islands. The rest are too dry and rocky for people to live on. Many people visit Greece for its beautiful beaches.

Crete is the largest of the Greek Islands.

Land

There are many mountains in Greece.

Mountains cover most of Greece. The biggest ones lie in the middle of Greece. There are a few small rivers, but these dry up in the hot summer.

coast

town

Most towns and cities in Greece are on the coast.

Most of the lower land is along the coasts.
This is where many of the towns and cities are.

Mount Olympus

Find Mount Olympus on page 4.

Mount Olympus is the highest mountain in Greece. It is 2917 metres high. The **Ancient** Greeks believed that gods lived on the top of Mount Olympus.

8

the Parthenon

the Acropolis

The Parthenon stands on a hill called the Acropolis.

Greece has many ancient buildings. The
Parthenon is one of the most famous. It stands
on a hill in Athens, called the Acropolis. The
Parthenon was built almost 2500 years ago as
a **temple** for Athena, the goddess of Athens.

9

Homes

blocks of flats

In Greek cities, most people live in flats.

Athens and Salonica are the two biggest cities in Greece. One-third of all Greeks live in or near Athens. Families live in small flats because the city is so crowded. Find Athens and Salonica on the map on page 4.

10

vine

356

Greeks paint the walls white to reflect the sun.

Most Greeks live in the country. Their homes usually have four or five rooms, flat roofs and white-washed walls. Greek houses often have **verandas**. **Vines** along the tops of the verandas give shade from the sun.

Food

fish

lobster

Seafood dishes are popular meals in Greece.

The Greeks eat a lot of **seafood** from the Mediterranean Sea. Some people like to buy their fish fresh from the harbours. The main meat eaten is lamb.

In summer, Greek people like to eat outside.

Lunch is the main meal of the day. Lunch is usually at about 2 p.m. Olive oil and many different herbs are used in Greek dishes. Lunch is often followed by an afternoon nap.

13

Clothes

black
shawls

Some older Greeks wear black clothes like these.

Most Greeks wear clothes like yours. Some older Greeks wear black when they go out. These women wear black shawls. They wear black clothes to show **respect** for members of the family who have died.

national dress

pompoms

This child is in Greek national dress.

The Greeks' **national** dress is a white shirt, red hat and white skirt. They wear pompoms on their shoes. Men, women and children wear this for special celebrations and dances.

Work

This farmer makes cheese out of the sheep's milk.

Many Greeks are farmers. They grow **crops** like wheat, tobacco, cotton, apples and grapes on the **plains** where the soil is good. Farmers also keep sheep and goats for their milk which is made into cheese.

Many tourists visit Greece every year.

Many Greeks work in the **tourist** industry because there are so many visitors to their country. They work in hotels, restaurants, shops and transport.

Transport

Donkeys can carry heavy loads on their backs.

People travel by **modern** and **old-fashioned** transport. On the **mainland**, people have cars and there are buses too. Many villages only have dirt tracks so donkeys are a good way of carrying heavy loads.

Ferries carry cars, buses, lorries and people between islands.

Greek shipping companies are famous around the world. Ships also ferry **tourists** between the Greek Islands or take them on cruises around the Mediterranean Sea. Ferries are used a lot around the Greek Islands.

Language

Most people in Greece speak Greek.

Most Greeks speak the Greek language. Greek is the oldest language spoken in **Europe**. Many Greeks also speak English. Some of our English words come from Greek.

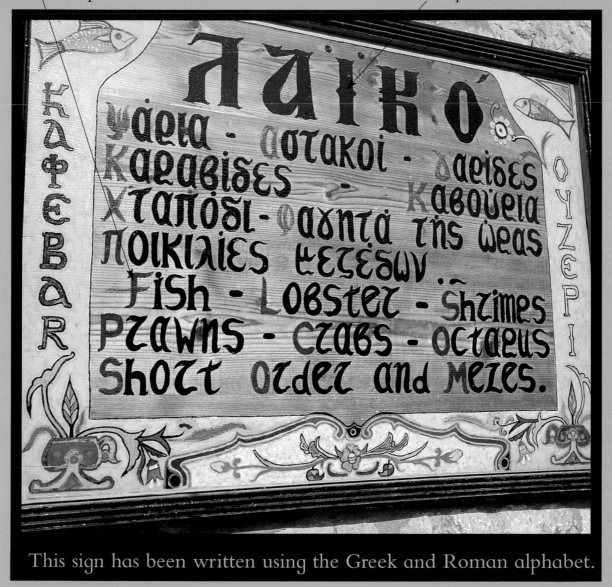

This sign has been written using the Greek and Roman alphabet.

Greek has its own alphabet of 24 letters. Many signs are written in both the Greek and **Roman** alphabets.

School

ΔΗΜΟΤΙΚΟ ΣΧΟΛΕΙΟ
≡ΜΥΚΟΝΟΥ≡

Greek flag

These children go to a Greek primary school.

Greek children go to school from the age of 6 to 15. They learn maths, art, music, religion, history and physical education. School starts at 8.30 a.m and finishes at 1.30 p.m.

These children have to study Greek in school.

Greek is the main language taught in school. Many children learn English or French, too.

Free time

Many people jump into the sea from the rocks for fun.

The first Olympic Games were held over 2000 years ago in 776 B.C. Today, almost all Greeks enjoy football (soccer), and swimming.

The first **modern** Olympics took place in Athens in 1896.

Kafeneions are popular places to meet friends.

The evening walk is a time for family and friends to chat. Adults also visit coffee-houses, called kafeneions, to play cards and meet their friends.

Celebrations

Priests lead big parades at religious festivals.

Easter is the most important festival in Greece. On Easter Day, church bells ring and people watch firework displays. The Greeks celebrate many other **religious** festivals, too.

traditional costumes

People celebrate festivals with singing and dancing.

At some festivals, the Greeks dress up in **traditional** costumes and celebrate with dancing and singing.

27

The Arts

stage
area

stone
seats

An ancient Greek theatre.

People have written and acted plays in Greece for over 2000 years. Today, both old and new plays are **performed** in the **ancient** theatres.

In Ancient Greece, men were the only actors. They wore masks to show which person they were playing.

This man is repairing a bouzouki.

The bouzouki is a Greek string instrument. Musicians play **traditional** songs on the bouzouki which are happy and sad at the same time.

Factfile

Name	The full name of Greece is the Hellenic Republic.
Capital	The **capital** city of Greece is Athens.
Languages	Most Greeks speak Greek and many can also speak a little English.
Population	There are about 10½ million people living in Greece.
Money	Instead of the dollar or pound, the Greeks have the drachma.
Religion	Most Greeks believe in Greek Orthodoxy which is part of the Christian church.
Products	Greece produces lots of olives and olive oil, cotton, grapes, tobacco, oil and some metals.

Words you can learn

enas (eh-nah)	one
dhio (theeoh)	two
tris (treace)	three
ya sis (yah-soos)	hello
andio (a-DEoh)	goodbye
efharisto (efkha-REE stoh)	thank you
parakalo (paraka-LOH)	please
ne (neh)	yes
ohi (okhi)	no

Glossary

ancient	from a long time ago
capital	the city where the government is based
crops	the plants that farmers grow
Europe	the collection of countries north of the Mediterranean Sea
mainland	a country's largest block of land
modern	new and up-to-date
national	shared by a nation or country
old-fashioned	from the past
performed	put on stage
plain	an area of flat, low land
religious	to do with people's beliefs
respect	to value someone or think highly of them
Roman	the type of letters which you read and write in English
seafood	fish and shellfish
temple	a place of worship
tourist	a person who travels to other countries for holidays
traditional	the way something has been done or made for a long time
veranda	long raised floor running along the front of a building
vine	a climbing plant, such as a grape

Index